Victorians

1837	Victoria becomes Queen
1840	January: the first postage stamps are issued February: Victoria marries Prince Albert of Saxe-Coburg
1842	It becomes illegal for women and children to work down mines
1850	Factory workers are allowed Saturday afternoons free
1851	The Great Exhibition
1854	The Crimean War begins
1856	Henry Bessemer invents steel The Crimean War ends
1861	Prince Albert dies of typhoid
1865	The first Salvation Army service takes place
1869	The first women's university college, Girton College, opens in Cambridge
1871	Henry Stanley finds David Livingstone in Africa
1877	1 January: Queen Victoria becomes Empress of India The first Test match is held between Britain and Australia
1880	Primary education becomes compulsory
1889	The first motor cars are built
1897	Queen Victoria's Diamond Jubilee
1901	22 January: the Queen dies

Victorians

Margaret Sharman

Chimnies swept by the Machine, if required.

M. GREEN,
(WIDOW OF THE LATE W. GREEN,)
No. 23, COLLONADE,
RUSSELL SQUARE;

Most respectfully informs the Nobility, Gentry and Customers in general, that she sweeps Chimnies and Flues of all descriptions in the best manner.

Small Boys for Register Stoves.

Widow Green earnestly hopes her customers will beware of certain persons, of bad characters, who make a practice of going about soliciting custom in her name, and procuring orders by saying they came from 23, COLLONADE. All orders directed as above, will be punctually attended to by your obedient Servant, **M. GREEN.**

☞ Night Work done on the shortest notice.

Peowrie and Nichoils, Printers, Milton-street, Finsbury.

Evans Brothers Limited

Published by
Evans Brothers Limited
2A Portman Mansions
Chiltern St
London W1U 6NR

Reprinted 2005, 2007, 2008

Printed in China

A catalogue record for this book is available from
the British Library.

ISBN 978 0 237 52573 6

Acknowledgements
Design: Ann Samuel
Editorial: Jill A.Laidlaw
Maps: Nick Hawken
Production: Jenny Mulvanny

Acknowledgements

For permission to reproduce copyright material,
the author and publishers gratefully acknowledge
the following:

Cover (main) The British Museum, (background)
the art archive, (top & middle) The Bridgeman Art
Library, (bottom) Mary Evans Picture Library. Title
page The Bridgeman Art Library. Contents page
Christie's Images, London. page 6 (top) Mary
Evans Picture Library, (bottom) The Bridgeman
Art Library. page 7 (top) Mary Evans Picture
Library, (bottom) The Bridgeman Art Library. page
8 Mary Evans Picture Library. page 9 the art
archive. page 10 (top) the art archive, (bottom)
The Bridgeman Art Library. page 11 (top) Mary
Evans Picture Library. page 12 The Bridgeman Art
Library. page 13 Mary Evans Picture Library. page
14 The Ancient Art & Architecture Collection.
pages 14-15 (bottom) Hulton Deutsch. page 15 The
Bridgeman Art Library. page 16 The Science
Museum/Science & Society Picture Library. page
17 (top) the art archive, (bottom) Hulton Deutsch.
page 18 (top) Mary Evans Picture Library, (bottom)
the art archive. page 19 Mary Evans Picture
Library. page 20 The Bridgeman Art Library. page
21 (top) the art archive/Tate Gallery, London,
(middle and bottom) Mary Evans Picture Library.
page 22 (top) Hulton Deutsch, (bottom) Christie's
Images. page 23 (top) The Bridgeman Art Library,
(bottom) Mary Evans Picture Library. page 24 the
art archive. page 25 (top) the art archive, (bottom
left and right) Mary Evans Picture Library. page 26
The Ancient Art & Architecture Collection, (bottom) The Bridgeman Art Library. page 27 (top)
Hulton Deutsch, (bottom) Mary Evans Picture
Library. page 28 (top) The Science
Museum/Science & Society Picture Library, (bottom) Hulton Deutsch. page 29 (top) The Science
Museum/Science & Society Picture Library, (bottom) The Bridgeman Art Library.

Contents

Sixty-four glorious years

Victoria was Queen of Great Britain for 64 years, from 1837 to 1901. Hers was the longest reign of any monarch in British history. We call British people of that time Victorians.

Queen Victoria

Victoria was a lonely child. Her father died when she was a baby and she had no brothers and sisters. She lived in Kensington Palace in London with her mother, who was German. Victoria never went to school but a German governess taught her German, French, history and arithmetic. She practised the piano and learnt to draw.

Victoria was never allowed to be alone – until 20 June, 1837, when she was 18. On that day her uncle, King William IV, died without a child to succeed him to the throne. At six o'clock in the morning the Archbishop of Canterbury and the Lord Chamberlain came to Victoria to tell her that she had become Queen of Great Britain.

A painting of Victoria and Albert with five of their nine children in 1846.

> I went into my sitting room (only in my dressing gown) and of course quite alone.
>
> Victoria's diary, 20 June, 1837

When Victoria was 20, she married her German cousin, Prince Albert, who was the same age. Albert became Victoria's chief advisor in affairs of state. Victoria and Albert had four sons and five daughters and were very happily married until Albert's death in 1861. Victoria was heartbroken at Albert's death and refused to go out in public for ten years. Victoria spent a great deal of her time in Scotland, at Balmoral Castle, a castle she had built to Albert's designs.

On 22 June 1897 people were given a special Bank Holiday to celebrate the Queen's Diamond Jubilee. People from all over the British Empire marched in a procession through London to give thanks for her 60 years on the throne.

This plate was made to celebrate the fiftieth anniversary of Victoria's reign in 1887.

Britain in 1837

When Victoria became Queen, Britain was mainly an agricultural nation, and most of its food was home-grown. In the industrial towns, men, women and children worked in cotton and woollen mills and factories. They worked from six o'clock in the morning to six or seven at night. They had no holidays, except Sundays.

If people wanted to travel they went by horse and cart or in a horse-drawn carriage. Private railways were only just beginning.

Britain by the 1890s

During Queen Victoria's reign millions of people moved from the countryside into towns. People became better educated (see pages 18-19) and healthier (see pages 24-5). Scientists made discoveries, such as how to prevent diseases spreading (see pages 24-5).

People were very proud of their Empire overseas (see pages 8-9) and thousands of Britons, particularly from Ireland and Scotland, emigrated to Australia, New Zealand and Canada (see page 17).

Railways were widely used by the 1890s by rich and poor alike.

A cartoon of Prime Minister William Gladstone in 1869 from a popular magazine.

Old friends, Victoria and Disraeli, walking together in 1887.

Victorian Prime Ministers

The queen or king is the Head of State and the Prime Minister is the head of the government.

The Liberal politician William Gladstone was Prime Minister four times during Victoria's reign. Gladstone started Post Office Savings Banks, so that workers could save a few pennies or shillings regularly. Gladstone supported the movement to get rid of the Act of Union (1801) which joined Ireland to Britain. He unsuccessfully tried to introduce Home Rule for Ireland in 1886 and 1893.

The Queen preferred the Conservative politician Benjamin Disraeli who was Prime Minister twice during her lifetime. Disraeli supported the Reform Act in 1867, which said that any man who lived at the same address for a year could vote at election time. Before this Act generally only rich men were allowed to vote. The Reform Act doubled the number of voters but women were still not allowed to vote. Disraeli was in favour of the Empire, and he persuaded Parliament to give the title 'Empress of India' to Victoria. On behalf of the Government he bought shares in the Suez Canal for Britain, so that British ships could sail safely and quickly to India and East Africa.

The British Empire

At the beginning of Victoria's reign, Great Britain governed parts of India, Canada, Australia and New Zealand, and had colonies in many other countries. A colony is a place ruled by immigrants from another nation. All the British colonies formed the British Empire.

The Empire grew throughout Victoria's reign and incorporated countries from the Far East and Africa. By 1901 it included countries, such as Kenya (British East Africa) and Northern Nigeria. Cecil Rhodes, Prime Minister of Cape Colony in South Africa, wanted the British to rule Africa from Cairo to Cape Town. He once said, 'I would annex the planets if I could!'. By 1901 nearly a quarter of all the people in the world were under British rule.

It's true!

The population of London increased from 2.3 million people in 1851 to four million by 1901. In 1851 one third of these people lived in poverty.

That enormous country, which is so bright a jewel of the Crown.

Queen Victoria writing about British India in 1877

This steamship of 1842 is typical of the British ships that travelled throughout the Empire carrying people and goods.

Settling in to new lands

The population of Britain expanded rapidly in the 19th century and towns such as London, Birmingham, Newcastle and Glasgow were overcrowded. Thousands of people left Britain for Australia, New Zealand or Canada. One reason people from Scotland and Ireland emigrated was to avoid starvation (see page 17).

The Empire brings wealth

In every colony British engineers built ports and native workmen built railways with tracks and engines imported from Britain. British farmers arrived in the colonies to farm the land, and they sent their produce by rail to the ports. British ships carried these goods to Britain. In return, the colonies imported goods from Britain such as clothes and blankets.

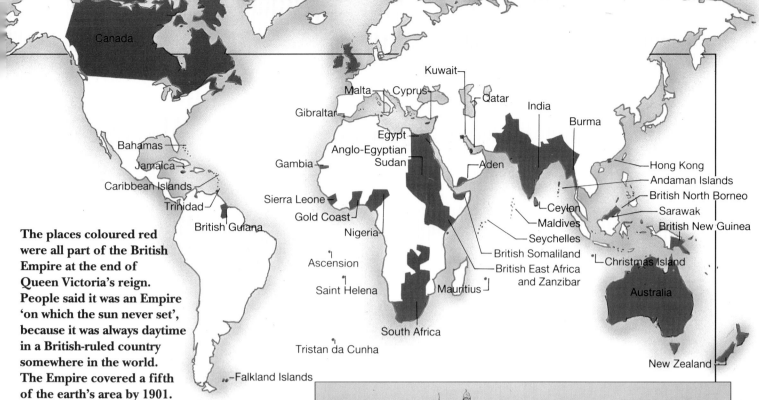

Canada

Kuwait
Malta — Cyprus
Gibraltar
Qatar
India
Burma
Egypt
Anglo-Egyptian
Bahamas
Sudan
Hong Kong
Jamaica
Gambia
Aden
Andaman Islands
Caribbean Islands
British North Borneo
Trinidad
Sierra Leone
Ceylon
Sarawak
Gold Coast
Maldives
British New Guinea
British Guiana
Nigeria
Seychelles
Ascension
British Somaliland
Christmas Island
British East Africa
and Zanzibar
Saint Helena
Mauritius
Australia
South Africa
Tristan da Cunha
New Zealand
Falkland Islands

The places coloured red were all part of the British Empire at the end of Queen Victoria's reign. People said it was an Empire 'on which the sun never set', because it was always daytime in a British-ruled country somewhere in the world. The Empire covered a fifth of the earth's area by 1901.

Teaching the British way of life

Throughout the Empire, British people built hospitals and British doctors and nurses went out to heal the sick. They trained local women to help in the wards. Missionaries travelled throughout the Empire teaching Christianity. They taught people to read, write, and speak English. These people were told to forget their own customs and religions. Today, people realise that forcing others to forget their culture was very destructive. But the Victorians believed that they were passing on the benefits of European civilisation to people whom they considered to be less fortunate.

The British army kept a regiment in every colony. Men from the colonies could join their own special divisions.

Hong Kong

The island of Hong Kong was a part of China which became a British colony in 1841. On this bare, rocky island, successful merchants built beautiful houses. Their warehouses were full of tea and silk from China, and the drug opium from India. Goods were sent to British ports in sailing ships called clippers. In 1898 Britain agreed to give Hong Kong back to the Chinese after 99 years, so it became part of China again in 1997.

Words, words, words ....

In October 1854 the British army fought the Russian army at a place called Balaclava during the Crimean War (1854-1856). The nights were very cold, and the soldiers wore woollen caps on their heads and over their ears to keep warm. They called these caps balaclavas.

Religion

The Church of England

The Church of England was then, as it is now, the official religion of Britain. It is a form of Protestant Christianity with the reigning monarch at its head. In 1837 Sunday church services could last for up to two and a half hours because preachers gave very long sermons. Many churches were uncared for, and some were even falling down. But the Victorians rebuilt churches and cleaned and decorated them. They filled the windows with stained glass, which was sometimes designed by famous Pre-Raphaelite painters (see pages 26-7). They installed organs, and some churches had a choir for the first time.

Nonconformists

Protestants who did not belong to the Church of England were called Nonconformists. In the industrial cities of the North and Midlands of England, many of the better paid workers went to Methodist chapels. Methodist preachers did not wear a special gown and the chapels were often converted barns or houses. In Wales, Methodist preachers spoke Welsh in chapel. The Methodists were concerned about human rights. They helped to ban the slave trade in Africa. In Britain, they worked to improve the lives of factory children.

Other Nonconformist groups such as the Baptists and the Quakers tended to be more like the Methodists in their worship of God than the Church of England.

Sunday at home

After the church service, Sunday was a quiet day for most people. Rich children were only allowed to read religious books and go for walks in their best clothes. Most of their toys were put away. Servants prepared the Sunday dinner on Saturday, so that they too could go to church.

For poor people, Sunday was their only day off work. Not many of them went to church. Wives cooked the family's weekly hot meal while the children played in the street. In the summer some families could listen to band music in the park.

A portrait of Victoria in stained glass, from a Norfolk church.

Children were allowed to play with Noah's Ark on Sundays because the story of Noah comes from the Bible.

The Salvation Army

In 1865 a Methodist called William Booth realised that going to a public house was the only entertainment working people could afford, as gin and porter (beer) were cheap. Booth held a Methodist service in the road outside a pub. Soon he had a band of people singing every Sunday. This was how the Salvation Army began. The Salvation Army helped poor people find food, clothes and shelter and this work continues today.

Missionaries

Ten thousand British men and women travelled to foreign lands as missionaries. Missionaries teach people to forget their own religion and follow the missionaries' religion — in this case Christianity. Some missionaries lived for years in huts all over the Empire without water or electric light and many died from tropical diseases. But in spite of all this, missionaries wrote down native languages for the first time and published dictionaries. They translated the Bible into over a hundred languages. For many years the schools and hospitals of the Empire were built and run by missionaries.

The men in white hats you can see in this photograph from 1900 are members of the Salvation Army. They are holding a service in a London street.

David Livingstone

In 1823 a ten-year-old Scot named David Livingstone started work in a cotton mill. He worked for 14 hours every day, and when work was over he taught himself all the subjects Scottish boys learnt at school. Livingstone studied hard enough to go to Medical School and then he became a missionary in southern Africa. He believed that Europeans should try to understand

This is the hat David Livingstone wore in Africa.

Africans – not just preach to them. In 1871 Livingstone had not been heard of for over a year. A Welsh journalist named Henry Morton Stanley was sent by an American newspaper to find Livingstone. After many months walking through 'bush' country (there were no proper roads), he found Livingstone at a place called Ujiji, in present-day Tanzania. He greeted the great missionary and explorer with the famous words, 'Dr Livingstone, I presume!'.

It's true!

In 1851 a survey revealed that only 35 per cent of people in England went to church on a Sunday.

Families at home

Prime Minister Benjamin Disraeli called Britain 'two nations'. One 'nation' consisted of people living comfortable lives. The poor, who worked for very low wages, made up the other 'nation'. The lives of these two groups of people were very different.

> Two nations... who are as ignorant of each other's habits, thoughts and feelings, as if they were dwellers in different zones, or inhabitants of different planets.
>
> Benjamin Disraeli in his novel Sybil, 1845

 Words, words, words ....

Mrs Beeton wrote 'a place for everything and everything in its place' in her book *Household Management*.

By looking at *The Dinner Party* by Henry Cole we can see how rich people ate and dressed when they entertained. Can you see the manservant in his special uniform?

The upper classes and middle classes

Wealthy people had large families looked after by large numbers of servants in large town houses. Mrs Beeton wrote a book called *Household Management* in 1859. She said that a man earning £1,000 a year should have a cook, a manservant, a nursemaid, and two housemaids. If he earned £200 a year, and rented a small house, he could still afford a maid to do all the work.

Very rich people had a coachman to drive their carriage and a groom who looked after the horses. Several gardeners kept the garden looking beautiful. The servants, though not very well paid, had good food to eat and warm clothes.

The children were looked after by a nursemaid. They played and had their meals in a day nursery and slept in a night nursery upstairs. Every evening they changed into clean clothes and went downstairs to see their parents for an hour. Often this was the only time the family was all together and the children had to be polite and quiet.

This is a Victorian scullery. A scullery was a room used for washing clothes and dishes. The mangle on the left was used to squeeze water out of wet clothes.

12

The working classes in towns

In the town centres, four or five families often lived in one house, or even in one room. Hardly any houses had an inside water tap. The lavatories, each shared by several families, were outside, in the back yards. Many terraced houses built for factory and mill workers had leaky roofs and damp walls. In every town horses pulled carriages and trams. The streets were full of horse manure and rubbish.

A train sends smoke over these crowded London houses in 1870. Several families lived in each home.

Few people could afford to send their children to school (see pages 18-19). Even infants of five or six were sent out to earn tiny wages. It all helped to pay the rent and the food bills. There was little left for clothes and boots. People were always cold in winter.

Old people with no money, orphans, and others who could not earn their own living were taken to a large unheated building called the workhouse. Everyone dreaded this happening to them. Husbands and wives were separated. During the day they had to sew sacks or unpick old stiff rope, which was used for making boats watertight. It was like being in prison for life.

The working classes in villages

Farm labourers did not have regular work and their wages were very low. There was no money for mending the roof, or putting in drains. Blacksmiths, wheelwrights, carpenters and harness-makers could afford better cottages. Everyone used horses to ride and to pull wagons, so these people had steady work.

Bath time!

On the village green, or in the town street, people filled buckets of water from the pump. People sometimes had a bath in a tin tub pulled up in front of the fire. It was filled with water heated on the stove. The whole family bathed, one after another. Victorian families could be large, so 10 or 12 people might share the same bath water!

It's true!

In one Suffolk workhouse in 1840, there was so little to eat that the inmates gnawed bones for nourishment. There were no toys in the workhouse until 1891, when the children were at last allowed to have skipping ropes.

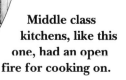

Middle class kitchens, like this one, had an open fire for cooking on.

Britain leads the way

A child trapper works down a mine.

The Industrial Revolution began in Britain in the 1760s when people started to invent machines that could do jobs that had always been done by hand. These machines were powered by steam. The steam was produced by boiling water over a very hot coal furnace.

Coal

Until about 1870, Britain produced half of all the coal mined in the world. For the first five years of Victoria's reign women and children worked with the men in the coal mines. They worked underground for 13 hours a day. Little children opened and closed ventilators (called 'trapping'), and older children dragged trucks of coal through tunnels. In 1842 the social reformer Lord Shaftesbury introduced an Act of Parliament that prevented women and children going down the mines.

It's true!

In 1851, 216,000 miners worked in the coal pits. Factories, houses and railway engines burned so much coal that thirty years later, in 1881, the mines employed 495,000 men!

> I have to trap without a light. It scares me. I don't like being in the pit
>
> Sarah Gooder, mineworker, aged eight, 1842

Cloth

Britain's second major industry was spinning and weaving cloth. Woollen cloth was woven in Leeds and Bradford. Manchester and neighbouring towns made cotton cloth. Before the cloth factories grew up, weaving had always been done in country homes by women working on their own looms. When people moved into the towns from the countryside women, and children from the age of nine or ten worked in the factories. In 1847 Parliament passed an Act that said people should only work for ten hours a day. This Act was also the work of Lord Shaftesbury. But people still worked in cramped mills, choking on the dusty cotton waste that floated in the air.

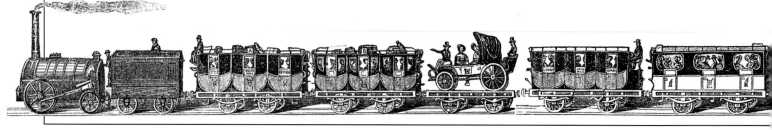

Iron and steel

Britain's third industry was iron working. In 1856 Henry Bessemer discovered how to make iron much harder by heating it in a furnace. The carbon in the iron melted and could be poured out of the bottom of the furnace to leave steel. Steel was used for making railway lines and engines, steam ships and factory machines. Birmingham and Sheffield produced small steel goods.

In 1851, in London, the Crystal Palace was built out of iron and glass. Here, Victoria opened the Great Exhibition – a display of 200,000 objects from all over the world.

T all chimneys, great uncouth shapes of kilns and furnaces appear through the smoke of a winter afternoon like turrets and pinnacles... Twilight and night are the conditions under which to see an iron-making town, the pillars of cloud by day, the pillars of fire by night.

Florence, Lady Bell, *At the Works*, written in the 1890s, published 1907

The railway boom

Railways were pioneered before Victoria's reign by George Stephenson and his son Robert. All through Victoria's reign people had to leave their homes to make way for new railway lines to be laid. The arrival of railways revolutionised transport. Railways were the first means of getting around the country quickly that people had ever known.

The greatest Victorian engineer was Isambard Kingdom Brunel. He designed railways, stations, bridges and viaducts. His largest steamship, the *Great Eastern*, was built in 1858 and could carry 4,000 passengers. It was five times bigger than any ship ever built and laid the first telegraph cable between Britain and the United States (see page 28). He designed the Clifton Suspension Bridge near Bristol, and Paddington Station in London. When he was only 29 he earned £2,000 a year, an enormous sum in Victorian times.

It's true!

Railway workmen (called 'navvies') each dug an average of 20 tonnes of earth a day as they tunnelled into hills and filled in valleys to make way for the railways. As many as 250,000 navvies laid railway tracks in 1848.

An early train with first and second class carriages for passengers. The third class wagons were for goods.

Living on the land

Before the 19th century, most people worked on the land. Much of the work was done by hand with ploughs pulled by horses. After steam-powered machines were invented farmers' work was changed for ever. Farmers used machines to sow the seed and harvest the corn. But these new machines did the job of several men so labourers had to look for jobs in the nearest town. This is how many country people became factory and mill workers.

A model of an early steam-powered plough. Many machines were invented to make farming easier.

Poor farmers

A poor farmer and his family lived simply. They ate the produce they had grown and the livestock they had tended. They drank beer brewed in their own farmhouses. The farmer's family worked long hours, with perhaps one or two casual labourers to help. The children scared away the birds from newly sown seed and removed stones from the fields. They looked after the lambs and collected the hens' eggs. At harvest time they helped the family bring in the corn.

My father earned only a shilling a day and... half a bag of oat flour cost us ten shillings and sixpence; therefore we could hardly afford bread, let alone anything to put on it.

Welsh worker's son in the 1880s, *Land of My Fathers*, Gwynfor Evans, 1974

A young girl milking the family cow as part of her daily chores on the farm.

Wales

Welsh sheep were bred for their meat and wool and cattle for their meat and hides. When the cattle were fat enough, men called drovers herded them through the mountains to England to be sold.

The Welsh had (and still have) their own language and culture. Often the landlords only spoke English. They did not understand Welsh or respect Welsh culture. This caused much resentment.

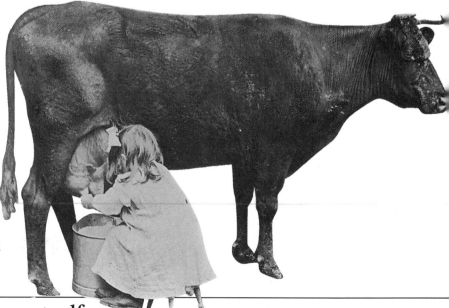

The Highland Clearances

Scottish farmers traditionally lived in small houses with a small amount of land (called a croft) rented from a wealthy landowner. But in the Highlands from the 1830s to 1860, landowners turned these poor farmers (called tenant farmers) out of their crofts to make way for sheep. English butchers paid a good price for Scottish mutton and so sheep farming was more profitable to the landowner than collecting rent from tenant farmers. Each farm only needed a few shepherds, so thousands of people were put out of their homes and jobs. Many Scottish families emigrated to America and Canada.

A British family has just arrived in Australia hoping to find their fortune. They have come to look for gold.

The Great Famine

Most of the land in Ireland was owned by Protestants and most of the land was farmed by Catholics. Agriculture was Ireland's biggest industry at the beginning of Victoria's reign. Tenant farmers grew potatoes, but even in good years, Irish peasants had only just enough food for their families. When the harvest failed they starved.

There was a great potato famine between 1845 and 1848, when perhaps as many as a million Irish people died of hunger. Those who lived had no money to pay the rent, even though it was only 1s. or 1s. 6d. a week (see pages 22-3), and were turned out of their homes. Many Irish people sailed to Britain to find work and over half a million of them emigrated to America.

It's true!

In 1851, 20.3 per cent of Britain's national income came from home-grown food. By 1901 agriculture only earned 6.4 per cent of Britain's national income. This is because by 1901 most of Britain's food was imported from the colonies.

Victims of the great potato famine in Ireland.

Words, words, words ....

Captain Boycott was a landlord's agent who turned Irish tenants who could not pay their rent out of their homes. Other tenants refused to move into the houses, so it was said that they 'boy-cotted' them. We still use this word today when we refuse to have anything to do with something we believe to be wrong.

Going to school

Education for poor children

At the beginning of the 19th century schools for poor children were run by the Church of England, local authorities, or charities. All of these schools taught 'the three Rs' – reading, (w)riting, and (a)rithmetic. Victorian school teachers liked their pupils to be respectful and hardworking, and caned them if they were not. Pupils were also taught a fourth 'R' – religion – and were expected to read the Bible and Prayer Book.

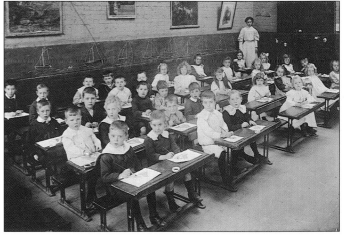

Boys and girls sat on opposite sides of the school-room. This is an art class.

In 1870 an Act of Parliament was passed which set up local education boards that were responsible for building new schools. Hundreds of new state schools were built. Some villages and towns still use these Victorian school rooms. They often have a little tower in which the school bell hung, two separate playgrounds for boys and girls and two doors into the school, one saying BOYS and the other GIRLS. But children did not have to go to school by law until 1880 and they had to pay for their education until 1891. Every Monday each pupil paid the teacher 4d. (see pages 22-3). This was not an expensive fee, but a labourer, earning perhaps 18 shillings a week, often could not pay this and then his child had to stay at home. Lord Shaftesbury was the chairman of an organisation that set up Sunday schools for very poor children. They were called Ragged Schools.

Children were allowed to leave school at 13 and very few went on to secondary school. Secondary schools taught Latin and Greek, history and religion, arithmetic and English. These were the subjects taught in universities.

It's true!

Around 1837 only very wealthy people could read and write. By 1901, 90 per cent of the population could read and write.

The pupils of a village school. Everyone wore boots rather than shoes.

Education for wealthy children

Boys whose parents could afford large fees for a public school such as Eton or Harrow learnt the same subjects as poor children. A few public schools taught science – but it was hard to find teachers or textbooks, as science was not a university subject until 1870. Teachers believed that games such as rugby, cricket and football taught a boy to be fair, to lead, and to follow a leader without question. These schools trained boys to govern Britain and the Empire.

Girls of wealthy parents were taught at home. The first girls' school in London taught more subjects than the boys' schools did, and had excellent teachers. From 1869 girls could go to women's colleges at Cambridge University.

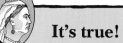

Reading for pleasure

There were no public libraries until the middle of the century because people who could read were rich enough to buy their own books. As more and more people learnt to read public libraries were opened under the Free Libraries Act of 1850. Newspapers such as *The Manchester Guardian, The Daily Telegraph* and *The Daily Mail* were founded. These new publications could be quickly transported around the country on the new railway network.

There was an Old Man on whose nose most birds of the air could repose;
But they all flew away at the closing of day,
Which relieved that Old Man and his nose.

Edward Lear (1812-1888) wrote *The Book of Nonsense*, with poems in it like the one above.

The explorer Mary Kingsley

Female explorers and doctors

During Victoria's reign women became more educated than at any previous time in British history. Educated women were able to break out of their traditional roles as wives and mothers and become explorers and doctors for the first time.

Mary Kingsley (1862-1900) travelled alone all over West Africa. Even in the most dangerous places she always dressed in a long black skirt and blouse and a fashionable hat! She frightened away crocodiles and hippos with her umbrella.

Sophia Jex-Blake wanted to become a doctor. No university accepted women, but she was so determined that in the end she was allowed to study in Edinburgh. Although she passed her exams in 1869, women were not allowed to practise medicine until 1894.

Elizabeth Garrett Anderson took her doctor's degree in Paris in 1870. Although not officially a doctor in Britain, she worked to improve the health of women and children.

The Victorians at leisure

It's true!

W. G. Grace played cricket for 45 years and during that time he scored 54,000 runs.

Victorian sport

Sporting events only became popular in about 1850, when public schools began to teach boys football, rugby and cricket. The most famous English cricketer was a bearded doctor called W.G. Grace (1848-1915), who made over a hundred centuries. At the end of Victoria's reign, the Indian prince and batsman, K.S. Ranjitsinhji, known as Ranji, played for Sussex and for the England team.

At first, football matches were very confusing because different clubs had different rules. The number of players was not fixed either so the Football Association made rules in 1848 which all clubs had to follow. Football then became a popular Saturday afternoon entertainment, as it is now.

Lawn tennis was only invented in 1874 and tennis clubs charged players about 5d. (see pages 22-3) for a two-hour game. The Wimbledon championships began in 1877. They were for men only, and the players faced a high net that dipped in the middle. Women, wearing long skirts and straw hats, began to play in 1884.

It's true!

After the Australians won the first Test match in 1877, the bails were burnt and put into a box. This was to show that English cricket had died! This trophy is called The Ashes and England and Australia still play each other to win them.

Family entertainment

When John Dunlop invented blow-up tyres in 1888, cycling became a craze. Before that there were heavy 'boneshaker' bikes with wooden wheels, and 'penny farthings', with the cyclist sitting on top of an enormous spoked wheel (the 'penny') balanced by a smaller one (the 'farthing'). Although there were tricycles for women, many girls rode proper bikes. They had to wear shorter skirts to avoid catching them in the wheel.

At the Music Hall adults laughed at comedians and joined in singing popular songs, which were often patriotic or rude!

Some wealthy people learnt to play the piano and to sing. They held after-dinner concerts in their drawing rooms. The Queen invited the German composer Felix Mendelssohn to play for her in 1847.

The wheels of this penny farthing bicycle are made of metal and have no tyres.

People also gave dance parties for their friends. The dances were mostly square dances, each square being made up of four couples. The dances had names like *The Quadrille* and *The Lancers*. Some older people were shocked to see their sons and daughters dashing round the floor dancing the waltz and the polka!

Dance quietly. Do not kick and caper about, nor sway your body to and fro. Dance only from the hips downwards.

A Victorian book of hints on how to behave, 1850s

People flocked to see wild animal shows and circuses. The American circus owner, Phineas T. Barnum, came to England in the 1870s with over a thousand performers and almost as many animals. Queen Victoria saw Barnum's show.

An afternoon at the seaside

After 1850 a new law allowed factories to close on Saturday afternoons so people started to go by train to the seaside during the summer. Women dressed themselves from head to toe in the water. Some even wore a corset made of rust-free metal! Men's swimming costumes often came up to the neck and down to the knee. Even children, riding donkeys or watching Punch and Judy shows, wore far more clothes on the beach than you would wear today.

These people are watching the Oxford and Cambridge boat race in 1862.

Going to the park to listen to a band was a popular family entertainment.

Punch and Judy puppet shows were always popular. Even though it is a sunny day these children are wearing plenty of clothes.

21

Everyday life

By the end of Victoria's reign people could buy food from all over the world in their local grocer's shop.

Going shopping

Britain's trade with her colonies increased during Victoria's reign. Town streets were lined with small shops that stocked goods from all over the world. In the grocers' shops there were cartons full of supplies such as dried fruit, biscuits and sugar, which you bought by the pound. The grocer also sold tinned meat from Argentina and tinned sardines from the Mediterranean. Greengrocers also supplied local vegetables and fruit.

In tea and coffee shops you could choose from a variety of types, or ask for a mixture of several blends. The shopkeeper weighed it and packed it up. Dairies sold milk, cheese and butter. The dairyman cut and weighed the butter for you. Milk came from the farm in a tall iron container called a milk churn. It was measured into a jug with an iron ladle.

Butchers hung their meat from great hooks in the shop window. Customers could buy beef from Scotland and lamb from Australia or New Zealand. They chose their fish from a fishmonger's marble slab. It had been brought by train from fishing ports such as Yarmouth. Fishing was a thriving industry, and fish were cheap.

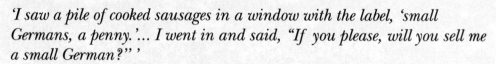

'I saw a pile of cooked sausages in a window with the label, 'small Germans, a penny.'... I went in and said, "If you please, will you sell me a small German?"'

Charles Dickens, *Household Words*, 1854

Here are two sides of the same penny coin. The pictures show the actual size of the penny.

Victorian money

A Victorian penny was divided into four farthings.

    2 farthings = 1 halfpenny (pronounced ha'penny)
    2 halfpennies = 1 penny
    12 pennies = 1 shilling
    20 shillings = 1 pound

For one penny people wrote 1d. (not 1p). If you wanted to write 'five pounds twelve shillings and sixpence', it looked either like this: £5 12s.6d., or like this £5/12/6.

People called £1/1/0 a guinea; a 5-shilling coin was called a crown and 2/6 was a half-a-crown. Gold pound coins were called sovereigns.

For a week's work a skilled worker, such as a bricklayer, earned about 25s.6d. An unskilled labourer earned about 18s. – not very much! A soldier's pay was only about 7s., but he had free food and lodging.

Self-employed street sellers

Many men and women made a living selling spices, flowers, cottons, medicines, matches and second-hand clothes. The muffin man walked round the streets with his barrow, and the knife-grinder knocked at doors asking for knives to sharpen. Crossing-sweepers earned a few pennies cleaning parts of the street, so that ladies could cross the road without getting their long skirts dirty. For poor people who worked all day in the factories and shops there were market stalls which sold hot pies, jellied eels and oysters. Oysters were very popular because they were cheap. They are much more expensive today and not many people can afford to eat them regularly.

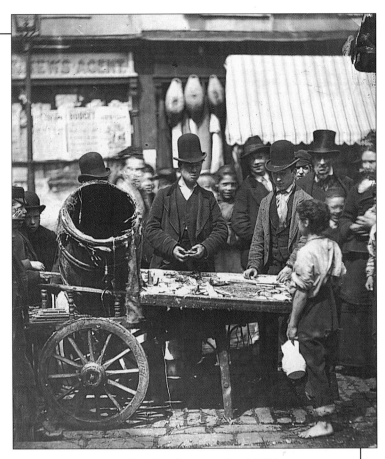

In this photograph of 1880 a street trader is selling fish. Notice that the men are all wearing hats.

Postage stamps

Sending letters was very expensive before stamps were invented – and the person receiving the letter had to pay for it. But in 1839 the sender could buy penny stamps (right) for the first time. After only one month the Post Office had to deal with twice the number of letters they usually handled! The first postcards appeared in 1870. They were plain, coloured cards printed with a stamp. Picture postcards only went on sale in 1894. All through Victoria's reign, postmen either walked or rode on horseback to deliver letters.

Today I sent my first postcards. They are capital things, simple, useful and handy. A happy invention.

Francis Kilvert, diarist, 4 October 1870

It's true!

In 1869 Mr and Mrs John James Sainsbury opened a little shop in London where they sold milk, eggs and butter. They were very successful, and they bought several other shop premises. Soon there were Sainsbury shops in many British towns selling all sorts of groceries. How pleased the Sainsburys would be to see that their shops have now become supermarkets!

In 1874 Jesse Boot started to sell herbal medicines in a little shop in Nottingham. He kept the quality of his goods high and his prices low. During the next 25 years over 160 other shops opened all over the country. This chain of shops is now called Boots the Chemists.

Health

Everyone, even people in well-fed families, expected at least one of their children to die young. At the beginning of Victoria's reign one child in every six died when it was born. More than half died before they were five years old. Hundreds of children suffered from scurvy, which caused their gums to swell and bleed. Scurvy was caused by a lack of vitamin C. Hundreds more had a disease called rickets, because they did not get enough vitamin D in their diet.

When all children had to go to school by law, teachers and doctors saw for the first time how many of them had crooked legs and spines (these are the effects of rickets), bad eyesight or hearing and rotten teeth. Without injections to protect them, children died of diphtheria (a disease which makes the throat swell and breathing hard), measles and chickenpox.

The disease people feared the most was tuberculosis, called consumption, which destroyed their lungs. Nobody knew what caused it, and there was no cure. In Glasgow in 1849, 4,000 people died of cholera, a disease which causes terrible pain in the stomach and fever. All over the country there were frequent outbreaks of both cholera and typhoid (another serious disease of the stomach with a high fever). These illnesses spread very quickly because of overcrowding and bad drainage. In every town, sewage went straight into the rivers, wells and streams which people drank from. In the 1880s a German doctor named Robert Koch discovered that consumption and cholera were caused by harmful bacteria found in polluted food and water.

A nurse inspecting a young girl's hair for head lice. Nurses were sent to schools to check children's health.

It's true!

In 1886 Members of Parliament held their noses and left the Parliament building because the smell from the River Thames was so bad they couldn't work. It was called the Great Stink.

Cleaning up the cities

People gradually began to realise that good living conditions were needed for good health. One man who studied the spread of disease was Sir Edwin Chadwick. By writing a book about his findings he persuaded Parliament to set up a Board of Health in 1848. As a result, huge sewer pipes, many of which we still use today, were buried beneath towns. House drains were then linked to them. The rivers became clearer and drinking water purer. A new reservoir supplied Glasgow with water, and in the next cholera epidemic only 53 people died there. More people than ever before had water taps fitted in their kitchens or back yards. But well into the 20th century workmen's cottages only had outside lavatories dug into the ground.

Florence Nightingale

In 1854, Florence Nightingale tended soldiers wounded in a war which Britain, France, Turkey and Sardinia fought against Russia, called the Crimean War. The high death rate in the soldiers' hospital at Scutari caused a scandal back in Britain. Florence, and the team of nurses she trained, made the wards clean and managed to reduce the death rate from 42 per cent to 2 per cent in just a year. Night after night she walked through the wards, and the soldiers called her 'the lady with the lamp'.

Florence spent the rest of her life working for better hospital conditions and training for nurses. Her work greatly improved public health and she was the founder of modern nursing.

Florence Nightingale is shown in this picture as the lady with the lamp at the hospital in Scutari.

We live in much filth... no privies (lavatories), no dustbins, no water supplies and no drain or sewer in the whole place... if the cholera comes Lord help us.

London workers' letter to *The Times*, 1849

Hospital improvements

Hospitals in 1837 were dark, cold and dirty. Patients lay on soiled beds, and nurses were often totally untrained. If a man or woman had an arm mangled by machinery, the doctor cut it off without any anaesthetic to make them unconscious. A surgeon was doing well if half his patients survived their operations. Then doctors discovered that they could use anaesthetics such as ether or chloroform to put patients to sleep before surgery.

Things gradually changed as doctors noticed how diseases spread in hospital wards. They started to use antiseptics and to scrub their hands before they operated on patients. New hospitals were built to treat the sick properly.

Study your Health for 5/-

MACKENZIE'S CLINICAL THERMOMETER.

For testing the Heat of the Body, showing the state of health, and if Influenza or Fever is present. As used by all Physicians, Doctors, and Private Families throughout the World. In Electro-Plated Cases, with Directions, Post Free 5s. each. WILL LAST A LIFETIME.
B. MACKENZIE, 31, Southampton Street, Strand, LONDON.

Doctors did not use thermometers until the 1870s. The thermometer we use today was invented in the 1880s.

Words, words, words ....

Many trades were dangerous to workers' health, and they were often poisoned by the chemicals they had to use. For instance, mercury had to be rubbed into felt by hand in hat making. The mercury would enter a hat maker's blood through his or her fingertips and sometimes cause brain damage. The fact that many hat makers went insane led to the common saying 'as mad as a hatter'.

This is an illustration of the Mad Hatter from Lewis Carroll's *Alice in Wonderland*.

The arts

An illustration from Charles Dickens' book *Nicholas Nickleby*, 1838. Nicholas is shown leaning over the desk writing.

The Pre-Raphelites painted scenes from stories and poems. This painting by John Everett Millais is of a scene from a poem by John Keats called *Isabella*.

Writers and poets

As more people learned to read, magazines, novels and travel books became popular. A favourite Victorian author was Charles Dickens (1812-1870). When he was 12 his father was put in prison because he could not pay his debts, and Charles had to work in a factory. So Dickens knew what kind of lives poor people led. His novels are full of interesting and amusing characters from all sections of British society.

The novels of Mrs Elizabeth Gaskell (1810-1865) describe the lives of cotton-mill workers. George Eliot (her real name was Mary Ann Evans) wrote *Middlemarch* (1871) and other novels about life in small towns changed by the arrival of the railway.

A Poet Laureate is the poet appointed to the monarch. Queen Victoria's laureates were, first, William Wordsworth (1770-1850), and then, Alfred Tennyson (1809-1892). Wordsworth wrote poems about the beauty of nature; Tennyson wrote romantic poems about King Arthur's knights, and a great religious poem called *In Memoriam*.

Artists

During Victoria's reign artists changed the way they painted the world around them. The Queen loved Edward Landseer's paintings of dogs and horses because they are so lifelike. Landseer sculpted the lions that guard Lord Nelson's statue in Trafalgar Square, London, in 1867. By contrast, Joseph Turner (1775-1851) painted pictures with few details but great atmosphere and colours.

By about 1850 a group of artists called the Pre-Raphaelite Brotherhood painted pictures of medieval history and legend. They were called Pre-Raphaelites because they painted in a style that was popular before (pre-) the time of the 15th-century Italian painter Raphael. Some of the most

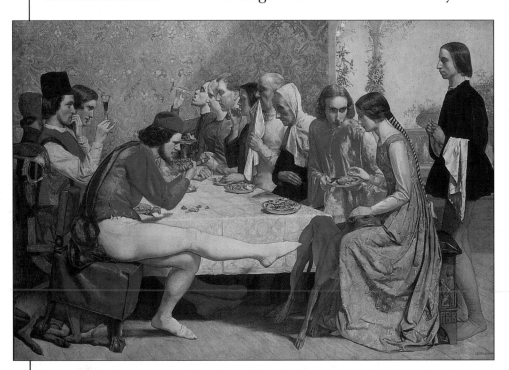

famous artists of this time were Dante Gabriel Rossetti, John Everett Millais, Edward Burne Jones, Holman Hunt, and William Morris. They also made books, stained glass, woodcuts and furniture.

Musicians

Every well-brought up girl was able to play the piano and both men and women could sing a little. During the 19th century concerts became popular. Charles Hallé started an orchestra in Manchester in 1858, and Sir Henry Wood conducted the first Promenade concert in London at the end of Victoria's reign. Classical music concerts were usually very expensive but Promenade concerts were meant to be cheap enough for poorer people to go to. Audiences loved the comic operas of Gilbert and Sullivan, which made fun of famous people. These operas of the 1870s-90s are still very popular today.

Manchester was a small country town in 1837. By the end of Victoria's reign it was one of the most important towns in Britain. The population had doubled with people working in the cotton mills. Manchester's Town Hall is built in the Gothic style (like the Houses of Parliament, bottom), while the Free Trade Hall (below) looks like an Italian building.

Architects

Sir George Gilbert Scott designed buildings and monuments in a medieval style (called Gothic), including the Albert Memorial in London (1863-1872), and Glasgow University. Augustus Pugin designed and decorated Gothic-style churches. Charles Barry liked the Italian style of architecture and he built many clubs and government buildings, including the Houses of Parliament from 1840 to 1860. Pugin made the Houses of Parliament look more Gothic by decorating the outside with details such as spires, dragons and lions.

The Houses of Parliament at the turn of the century

Science and technology

The Victorians were great scientists and inventors. We have seen how they invented steamships, steel and bicycles. Imagine what it would have felt like to experience these things for the first time, as Queen Victoria did! Here are some more of the inventions and ideas that changed people's lives.

The camera

Family portraits were very popular. Cameras were big and heavy, and the shutter moved very slowly. The sitter had to stay very still for up to ten seconds, otherwise the photograph came out blurred. This is why people do not smile in early photographs – it was too difficult to keep smiling for such a long time. Photographers put the camera on a tripod to avoid shaking it and then they covered their heads and the sides of the camera with a black cloth to take the photograph. In 1889 the first box cameras went on sale in the shops, and people could at last take snapshots.

The British inventor Joseph Wilson Swan invented this electric light bulb.

The telegraph

Messages were sent in dots and dashes (Morse Code) from a transmitter in one place to a receiver in another. The message travelled along wires. In 1858 a person in Wales could send such a message to Ireland. The wires were enclosed in a cable under the sea. Eight years later a cable was laid under the Atlantic from Britain to America by Brunel's steamship the *Great Eastern*.

The telephone

In 1876 Alexander Graham Bell, a Scot living in America, invented the telephone when he discovered how to make sound travel along wires. The first words spoken by telephone were: 'Mr Watson, come here. I want you', when Bell spoke to his assistant.

Alexander Bell making the first phone call from New York to Chicago in 1892.

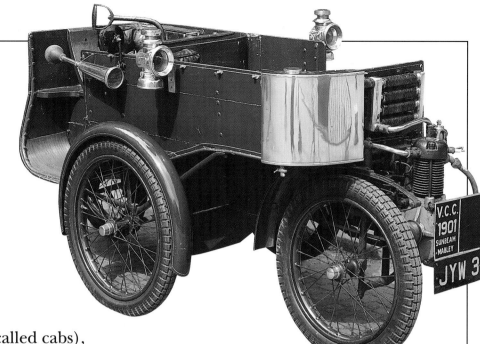

One of the first cars, the *Sunbeam*, of 1901. It had only three wheels. The driver sat at the back and steered the car by a lever.

Motor cars

Horses pulled carriages, taxis (called cabs), buses and carts for most of Victoria's reign. So when cars with petrol engines were invented in 1889, they were called 'horseless carriages'. The tyres were made of solid rubber, which made cars quite uncomfortable. The speed limit was 4 miles per hour (roughly 6 kilometres per hour) in the country and 2 miles per hour (roughly 3 kilometres per hour) in the town – and a man had to walk in front of the car waving a red flag. In 1896 the speed limit was raised to 20 miles per hour (roughly 32 kilometres per hour).

The Automobile Association (AA) was founded in 1897. Patrolmen warned their members of police speed traps ahead! At the beginning of the new century motorbikes went on sale.

A cartoon of Darwin from 1874 which makes fun of his theory of evolution.

Evolution

The Victorians believed that God created one man, Adam, and one woman, Eve, and all the rest of the world in seven days. In 1859 Charles Darwin wrote a book called *On the Origin of Species*, in which he said that all the animals and plants we know today were quite different millions of years ago. Darwin called this process of change evolution. Darwin's theory explains that some species of animals and plants become extinct because they do not adapt to their changing surroundings. Other animals and plants change and adapt to their environment in order to survive. In this way humans evolved from ape-like creatures. Darwin's book offended many people because it said that God did not create the world in seven days but that it evolved over millions of years.

M*an with all his noble qualities... still bears in his bodily frame the indelible* (permanent) *stamp of his lowly origin.*

Charles Darwin writing about evolution, 1871

Index

Glossary

addict   a person who is unable to stop a habit (such as smoking)

agent   someone who acts on behalf of an employer

annex   to take possession of territory

antiseptic   liquid or cream which stops harmful bacteria spreading

bails   short wooden bars put across the wicket in the game of cricket

casual labourer   someone who does not have permanent employment

century   (in cricket) one hundred runs

chloroform   a colourless liquid, which makes the mind and body fall asleep when its fumes are breathed in

commuter   someone who travels to work and back every day by public or private transport

Diamond Jubilee   the sixtieth anniversary of the day Victoria became Queen

emigrate   to leave your native country to settle in another

ether   a liquid which makes the mind and body fall asleep when its fumes are breathed in

furnace   a closed fire which can reach a very high temperature

Lord Chamberlain   the chief court official

Lord Nelson (1758-1805)   a British naval commander who fought the French in the Napoleonic wars

monarch   a king or queen

opium   an addictive drug made from unripe poppy seeds

overdose   too much of a medicine or drug

patriotic   being proud of one's country

social reformer   someone who attempts to improve the lives of underprivileged people

Suez Canal   a canal that crosses north-east Egypt to link the Mediterranean Sea with the Red Sea

Test match   one of a series of cricket matches between different countries

viaduct   a long bridge made up of arches, crossing a valley

Places to visit

There are many museums in towns and cities throughout Britain where you can see things made during Victorian times. Look around your own area for Victorian buildings, railway stations, libraries, schools and shops. Look at the list below to see where you can visit some Victorian sites.

London
The Victoria and Albert Museum, South Kensington, SW7
The Science Museum, South Kensington, SW7
Bethnal Green Museum of Childhood, E2
The Imperial War Museum, SE1
The London Transport Museum, WC2
The National Maritime Museum, Greenwich, SE10
The Museum of London, EC2
Dickens House Museum and Library, 48 Doughty Street, WC1

West and south-west England
Museum of English Rural Life, Reading University
Great Western Railway Museum, Swindon
Railway Village Museum, Swindon
Ironbridge Gorge Visitors' Centre, Ironbridge, Shropshire
Shambles Museum, Newent, Gloucester
Bath Industrial Heritage Centre, Bath, Avon
Museum of Costume, Bath, Avon
Flambards Village theme park, Helston
Tintagel Old Post Office, Tintagel, Cornwall

South and south-east England
Peterborough Museum and Art Gallery, Peterborough
Hitchin Museum and Art Gallery
Cambridge and County Folk Museum, Cambridge
Strangers' Hall, Norwich
Tide Mill, Woodbridge, Suffolk
The Royal Navy Museum, Portsmouth
Osbourne House, Isle of Wright
Hardy's Wessex Exhibition, Dorchester

North-west England and the Midlands
Brewery Museum, Stamford, Lincolnshire
Warwick Castle, Warwick
Lock Museum, Willenhall
Southport Railway Centre, Southport, Merseyside
Keswick Museum and Art Gallery, Cumbria
Windermere Steamboat Museum, Bowness-on-Windermere, Cumbria

North and north-east England
The Darlington Railway Centre, Darlington
Timothy Hackworth Victorian Railway Museum, Shieldon, Durham
Open Air Museum, Beamish, Durham
Bowes Museum, Barnard Castle, Durham
National Railway Museum, York
Castle Museum, York
Industrial Museum, Bradford, West Yorkshire
Abbey House Museum, Leeds

Scotland
The Angus Folk Museum, Angus, Glamis, Tayside
Scottish Fisheries Museum, Anstruther, Fife
Lady Stairs House, Edinburgh
Old Byr Heritage Centre, Dervaig, Isle of Mull
Gladstone Court Museum, Biggar, Strathclyde
Museum of Childhood, Edinburgh
Kelvingrove Art Gallery, Glasgow
National Gallery of Scotland, Edinburgh

Wales
Welsh Folk Museum, St Fagans, Cardiff
Welsh Industrial and Maritime Museum
Conwy Valley Railway Museum, Betws-y-Coed, Gwynedd
Beaumaris Gaol and Court, Llangefni, Gwynedd
The Lloyd George Museum and Highgate, Criccieth, Gwynedd
Llechwedd Slate Caverns, Blaenau Ffestiniog, Gwynedd
Bobelwyddan Castle, Clwyd
Alice in Wonderland Visitor Centre, Llandudno, Gwynedd
Horse-Drawn Boats and Canal Exhibition Centre, Llangollen, Clwyd
Rhondda Heritage Park, Trehafod, Mid Glamorgan
Victorian School of the Three Rs, Llangollen, Clwyd

Northern Ireland
Malone House, Belfast
Palm House and Tropical Ravine, Belfast
Crown Loquer Saloon, Belfast
Benburb Valley Heritage Centre, County Tyrone
Gray's Printing Press, County Tyrone
Carrickfergus Gasworks, County Antrim
The Argory, County Armagh
Ballycopeland Windmill, County Down
Castle Ward, County Down